MW00962173

ISBN: 9798743667062

Copyright © 2021

PARK NAME	CITY	COUNTY	VISITED
Abilene State Park	Tuscola	Taylor	
Atlanta State Park	Atlanta	Cass	
Balmorhea State Park	Toyahvale	Reeves	
Barton Warnock Visitor Center	Terlingua	Brewster	
Bastrop State Park	Bastrop	Bastrop	
Battleship Texas State Historic Site	LaPorte	Harris	
Bentsen-Rio Grande Valley State Park	Mission	Hidalgo	
Big Bend Ranch State Park	Marfa	Presidio, Brewster	
Big Spring State Park	Big Spring	Howard	
Blanco State Park	Blanco	Blanco	
Bonham State Park	Bonham	Fannin	
Brazos Bend State Park	Needville	Fort Bend	
Buescher State Park	Smithville	Bastrop	
Caddo Lake State Park	Karnack	Harrison	
Caprock Canyons State Park & Trailway	Quitaque	Briscoe	
Cedar Hill State Park	Cedar Hill	Dallas	
Choke Canyon State Park	Calliham	Live Oak, McMullen	
Cleburne State Park	Cleburne	Johnson	
Colorado Bend State Park	Bend	Lampasas, San Saba	
Cooper Lake State Park	Cooper	Cooper	
Copper Breaks State Park	Quanah	Hardeman	
Daingerfield State Park	Daingerfield	Morris	
Davis Mountains State Park	Fort Davis	Davis	
Devils River State Natural Area	Del Rio	Val Verde	
Devil's Sinkhole State Natural Area	Rocksprings	Edwards	
Dinosaur Valley State Park	Glen Rose	Somervell	
Eisenhower State Park	Denison	Grayson	
Enchanted Rock State Natural Area	Fredericksburg	Llano	

PARK NAME	CITY	COUNTY	VISITED
Estero Llano Grande State Park	Weslaco	Hidalgo	
Fairfield Lake State Park	Fairfield	Freestone	
Falcon State Park	Falcon Heights	Zapata, Starr	
Fort Boggy State Park	Centerville	Leon	
Fort Leaton State Historic Site	Presidio	Presidio	
Fort Parker State Park	Mexia	Limestone	
Fort Richardson State Park & Historic Site / Lost Creek Reservoir State Trailway	Jacksboro	Jack	
Franklin Mountains State Park	El Paso	El Paso	
Galveston Island State Park	Galveston	Galveston	
Garner State Park	Concan	Uvalde	
Goliad State Park & Historic Site	Goliad	Goliad	
Goose Island State Park	Rockport	Aransas	
Government Canyon State Natural Area	San Antonio	Bexar	
Guadalupe River State Park	Spring Branch	Comall, Kendall	
Hill Country State Natural Area	Bandera	Bandera, Medina	
Honey Creek State Natural Area	Spring Branch	Comal	
Hueco Tanks State Park & Historic Site	El Paso	El Paso	
Huntsville State Park	Huntsville	Walker	
Indian Lodge	Fort Davis	Jeff Davis	
Inks Lake State Park	Burnet	Burnet	
Kickapoo Cavern State Park	Brackettville	Kinney, Edwards	
Lake Arrowhead State Park	Wichita Falls	Clay	
Lake Bob Sandlin State Park	Pittsburg	Titus, Camp, Franklin	
Lake Brownwood State Park	Lake Brownwood	Brown	
Lake Casa Blanca International State Park	Laredo	Webb	
Lake Colorado City State Park	Colorado City	Mitchell	
Lake Corpus Christi State Park	Mathis	San Patricio	
Lake Livingston State Park	Livingston	Polk	

PARK NAME	CITY	COUNTY	VISITED
Lake Mineral Wells State Park & Trailway	Mineral Wells	Parker	
Lake Somerville State Park & Trailway	Somerville	Burleson, Lee	
Lake Tawakoni State Park	Wills Point	Hunt	
Lake Whitney State Park	Whitney	Hill	
Lockhart State Park	Lockhart	Caldwell	
Longhorn Cavern State Park	Burnet	Burnet	
Lost Maples State Natural Area	Vanderpool	Bandera, Real	
Lyndon B. Johnson State Park & Historic Site	Stonewall	Gillespie	
Martin Creek Lake State Park	Tatum	Rusk	
Martin Dies, Jr. State Park	Jasper	Jasper, Tyler	
Mckinney Falls State Park	Austin	Travis	
Meridian State Park	Meridian	Bosque	
Mission Tejas State Park	Grapeland	Houston	
Monahans Sandhills State Park	Monahans	Ward, Winkler	
Mother Neff State Park	Moody	Coryell	
Mustang Island State Park	Corpus Christi	Nueces	
Old Tunnel State Park	Fredericksburg	Kendall	
Palmetto State Park	Gonzales	Gonzales	
Palo Duro Canyon State Park	Canyon	Randall	
Pedernales Falls State Park	Johnson City	Blanco	
Possum Kingdom State Park	Caddo	Palo Pinto	
Purtis Creek State Park	Eustace	Henderson, Van Zandt	
Ray Roberts Lake State Park	Pilot Point	Denton, Cooke, Grayson	
Resaca de la Palma State Park	Brownsville	Cameron	
San Angelo State Park	San Angelo	Tom Green	
Sea Rim State Park	Sabine Pass	Jefferson	
Seminole Canyon State Park & Historic Site	Comstock	Val Verde	
Sheldon Lake State Park & Environmental Learning Center	Houston	Harris	

PARK NAME	CITY	COUNTY	VISITED
South Llano River State Park	Junction	Kimble	
Stephen F. Austin State Park	San Felipe	Austin	
Tyler State Park	Tyler	Smith	
Village Creek State Park	Lumberton	Hardin	
Wyler Aerial Tramway	El Paso	El Paso	

COUNTY	PARK NAME	EST.	VISITED
Aransas	Goose Island State Park	1935	
Austin	Stephen F. Austin State Park	1940	
Bandera, Medina	Hill Country State Natural Area	1984	
Bandera, Real	Lost Maples State Natural Area	1979	
Bastrop	Bastrop State Park	1937	
Bastrop	Buescher State Park	1940	
Bexar	Government Canyon State Natural Area	1993	
Blanco	Government Canyon State Natural Area	1934	
Blanco	Pedernales Falls State Park	1971	
Bosque	Meridian State Park	1935	
Brewster	Barton Warnock Visitor Center	1990	
Briscoe	Caprock Canyons State Park & Trailway	1982	
Brown	Lake Brownwood State Park	1938	
Burleson, Lee	Lake Somerville State Park & Trailway	1970	
Burnet	Inks Lake State Park	1950	
Burnet	Longhorn Cavern State Park	1976	
Caldwell	Lockhart State Park	1948	
Cameron	Resaca de la Palma State Park	2008	
Cass	Atlanta State Park	1954	
Clay	Lake Arrowhead State Park	1970	
Comal	Honey Creek State Natural Area	1985	
Comall, Kendall	Guadalupe River State Park	1983	
Cooper	Cooper Lake State Park	1992	
Coryell	Mother Neff State Park	1937	
Dallas	Cedar Hill State Park	1982	
Davis	Davis Mountains State Park	1938	
Denton, Cooke, Grayson	Ray Roberts Lake State Park	1993	
Edwards	Devil's Sinkhole State Natural Area	1985	

COUNTY	PARK NAME	EST.	VISITED
El Paso	Franklin Mountains State Park	1987	
El Paso	Hueco Tanks State Park & Historic Site	1970	
El Paso	Wyler Aerial Tramway	2001	
Fannin	Bonham State Park	1933	
Fort Bend	Brazos Bend State Park	1984	
Freestone	Fairfield Lake State Park	1976	
Galveston	Galveston Island State Park	1975	
Gillespie	Lyndon B. Johnson State Park & Historic Site	1965	
Goliad	Goliad State Park & Historic Site	1936	
Gonzales	Palmetto State Park	1936	
Grayson	Eisenhower State Park	1954	
Hardeman	Copper Breaks State Park	1974	
Hardin	Village Creek State Park	1994	
Harris	Battleship Texas State Historic Site	1948	
Harris	Sheldon Lake State Park & Environmental Learning Center	1984	
Harrison	Caddo Lake State Park	1933	
Henderson, Van Zandt	Purtis Creek State Park	1988	
Hidalgo	Bentsen-Rio Grande Valley State Park	1944	
Hidalgo	Estero Llano Grande State Park	2006	
Hill	Lake Whitney State Park	1965	
Houston	Mission Tejas State Park	1957	
Howard	Big Spring State Park	1936	
Hunt	Lake Tawakoni State Park	1984	
Jack	Fort Richardson State Park & Historic Site / Lost Creek Reservoir State Trailway	1968	
Jasper, Tyler	Martin Dies, Jr. State Park	1965	
Jeff Davis	Indian Lodge	1939	
Jefferson	Sea Rim State Park	1977	
Johnson	Cleburne State Park	1938	

COUNTY	PARK NAME	EST.	VISITED
Kendall	Old Tunnel State Park	2012	
Kimble	South Llano River State Park	1990	
Kinney, Edwards	Kickapoo Cavern State Park	1991	
Lampasas, San Saba	Colorado Bend State Park	1987	
Leon	Fort Boggy State Park	1985	
Limestone	Fort Parker State Park	1941	
Live Oak, McMullen	Choke Canyon State Park	1987	
Llano	Enchanted Rock State Natural Area	1978	
Mitchell	Lake Colorado City State Park	1972	
Morris	Daingerfield State Park	1938	
Nueces	Mustang Island State Park	1979	
Palo Pinto	Possum Kingdom State Park	1940	
Parker	Lake Mineral Wells State Park & Trailway	1981	
Polk	Lake Livingston State Park	1977	
Presidio	Fort Leaton State Historic Site	1973	
Presidio, Brewster	Big Bend Ranch State Park	1988	
Randall	Palo Duro Canyon State Park	1934	
Reeves	Balmorhea State Park	1968	
Rusk	Martin Creek Lake State Park	1976	
San Patricio	Lake Corpus Christi State Park	1934	
Smith	Tyler State Park	1939	
Somervell	Dinosaur Valley State Park	1972	
Taylor	Abilene State Park	1933	
Titus, Camp, Franklin	Lake Bob Sandlin State Park	1987	
Tom Green	San Angelo State Park	1995	
Travis	Mckinney Falls State Park	1976	
Uvalde	Garner State Park	1941	
Val Verde	Devils River State Natural Area	1988	

COUNTY	PARK NAME	EST.	VISITED
Val Verde	Seminole Canyon State Park & Historic Site	1980	
Walker	Huntsville State Park	1956	
Ward, Winkler	Monahans Sandhills State Park	1957	
Webb	Lake Casa Blanca International State Park	1991	
Zapata, Starr	Falcon State Park	1965	

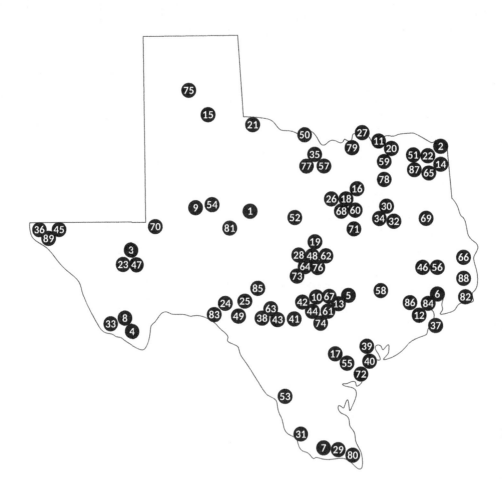

1. Abilene State Park
2. Atlanta State Park
3. Balmorhea State Park
4. Barton Warnock Visitor Center
5. Bastrop State Park
6. Battleship Texas State Historic Site
7. Bentsen-Rio Grande Valley State Park
8. Big Bend Ranch State Park
9. Big Spring State Park
10. Blanco State Park
11. Bonham State Park
12. Brazos Bend State Park
13. Buescher State Park
14. Caddo Lake State Park
15. Caprock Canyons State Park & Trailway
16. Cedar Hill State Park
17. Choke Canyon State Park
18. Cleburne State Park
19. Colorado Bend State Park
20. Cooper Lake State Park
21. Copper Breaks State Park
22. Daingerfield State Park
23. Davis Mountains State Park
24. Devils River State Natural Area
25. Devil's Sinkhole State Natural Area
26. Dinosaur Valley State Park
27. Eisenhower State Park
28. Enchanted Rock State Natural Area
29. Estero Llano Grande State Park
30. Fairfield Lake State Park
31. Falcon State Park
32. Fort Boggy State Park
33. Fort Leaton State Historic Site
34. Fort Parker State Park
35. Fort Richardson State Park & Historic Site / Lost Creek Reservoir State Trailway
36. Franklin Mountains State Park
37. Galveston Island State Park
38. Garner State Park
39. Goliad State Park & Historic Site
40. Goose Island State Park
41. Government Canyon State Natural Area
42. Guadalupe River State Park
43. Hill Country State Natural Area
44. Honey Creek State Natural Area
45. Hueco Tanks State Park & Historic Site
46. Huntsville State Park
47. Indian Lodge
48. Inks Lake State Park
49. Kickapoo Cavern State Park
50. Lake Arrowhead State Park
51. Lake Bob Sandlin State Park
52. Lake Brownwood State Park
53. Lake Casa Blanca International State Park
54. Lake Colorado City State Park
55. Lake Corpus Christi State Park
56. Lake Livingston State Park
57. Lake Mineral Wells State Park & Trailway
58. Lake Somerville State Park & Trailway
59. Lake Tawakoni State Park
60. Lake Whitney State Park
61. Lockhart State Park
62. Longhorn Cavern State Park
63. Lost Maples State Natural Area
64. Lyndon B. Johnson State Park & Historic Site
65. Martin Creek Lake State Park
66. Martin Dies, Jr. State Park
67. Mckinney Falls State Park
68. Meridian State Park
69. Mission Tejas State Park
70. Monahans Sandhills State Park
71. Mother Neff State Park
72. Mustang Island State Park
73. Old Tunnel State Park
74. Palmetto State Park
75. Palo Duro Canyon State Park
76. Pedernales Falls State Park

77 Possum Kingdom State Park

78 Purtis Creek State Park

79 Ray Roberts Lake State Park

80 Resaca de la Palma State Park

81 San Angelo State Park

82 Sea Rim State Park

83 Seminole Canyon State Park & Historic Site

84 Sheldon Lake State Park & Environmental Learning Center

85 South Llano River State Park

86 Stephen F. Austin State Park

87 Tyler State Park

88 Village Creek State Park

89 Wyler Aerial Tramway

INVENTORY

- BEAR SPRAY
- BINOCULARS
- CAMERA + ACCESSORIES
- CELL PHONE + CHARGER
- FIRST AID KIT
- FLASHLIGHT/ HEADLAMP
- FLEECE/ WATERPROOF JACKET
- GUIDE BOOK
- HAND LOTION
- HAND SANITIZER
- HIKING SHOES
- INSECT REPELLENT
- LIP BALM
- MEDICATIONS AND PAINKILLERS
- NATIONAL PARK MAP
- NATIONAL PARK PASS
- SUNGLASSES
- SNACKS
- SPARE SOCKS
- SUN HAT
- SUNSCREEN
- TOILET PAPER
- TRASH BAGS
- WALKING STICK
- WATER
- WATER SHOES/ SANDALS

ABILENE STATE PARK

COUNTY: TAYLOR   **ESTABLISHED:** 1933   **AREA (AC/HA):** 530 / 214

DATE(S) VISITED: SPRING ☐   SUMMER ☐   FALL ☐   WINTER ☐

WEATHER: ☀ ☐ ☁ ☐ ☔ ☐ ❄ ☐ 🌧 ☐ 🌬 ☐   **TEMP.:**

FEE(S):   RATING: ☆ ☆ ☆ ☆ ☆   **WILL I RETURN?**   YES / NO

LODGING: **WHO I WENT WITH:**

THINGS TO DO: CAMP, HIKE, GEOCACHE, BIRD WATCH, BIKE, SWIM, FISH, BOAT

POPULAR ATTRACTIONS:

- Historic Swimming Pool, built in the early 1930s by the Civilian Conservation Corps.
- Stone Water Tower.
- The Grace Museum.
- Paramount Theatre.
- Trampoline Park.
- Zoo.
- 12th Armored Division Memorial.
- National Center for Children's Ilustrated Literature.

NOTES:

PASSPORT STAMPS

ATLANTA STATE PARK

COUNTY: CASS   **ESTABLISHED:** 1954   **AREA (AC/HA):** 1,475 / 597

DATE(S) VISITED: SPRING ☐   SUMMER ☐   FALL ☐   WINTER ☐

WEATHER: ☀☐ ⛅☐ 🌧☐ ❄☐ ⛈☐ 🌫☐   **TEMP.:**

FEE(S):   RATING: ☆ ☆ ☆ ☆ ☆   **WILL I RETURN?** YES / NO

LODGING: **WHO I WENT WITH:**

THINGS TO DO: CAMP, HIKE, GEOCACHE, BIRD WATCH, BIKE, SWIM, FISH, BOAT

POPULAR ATTRACTIONS:

- Riding a Narrow-Gauge Train.
- River Boat.
- Rodeo.
- Wildflower Festival.

NOTES:

PASSPORT STAMPS

BALMORHEA STATE PARK

COUNTY: REEVES   **ESTABLISHED:** 1968   **AREA (AC/HA):** 751 / 304

DATE(S) VISITED: SPRING ☐   SUMMER ☐   FALL ☐   WINTER ☐

WEATHER: ☀☐   ⛅☐   🌧☐   ❄☐   ⛈☐   🌫☐   **TEMP.:**

FEE(S):   RATING: ☆ ☆ ☆ ☆ ☆   **WILL I RETURN?** YES / NO

LODGING: **WHO I WENT WITH:**

THINGS TO DO: CAMP, HIKE, GEOCACHE, BIRD WATCH, SKIN DIVE, SWIM, FISH, BOAT, SCUBA

POPULAR ATTRACTIONS:

- McDonald Observatory.
- Replica of Judge Roy Bean's West of the Pecos Museum.
- Chihuahuan Desert Research Institute.
- Sul Ross State University.
- Museum of the Big Bend.
- Anne Riggs Museum.
- Rooney Park.

NOTES:

PASSPORT STAMPS

BARTON WARNOCK VISITOR CENTER

COUNTY: BREWSTER   **ESTABLISHED:** 1990   **AREA (AC/HA):** 100 / 40

DATE(S) VISITED: SPRING ☐   SUMMER ☐   FALL ☐   WINTER ☐

WEATHER: ☀☐ ⛅☐ 🌧☐ ❄☐ 🌧☐ 🌬☐   **TEMP.:**

FEE(S):   RATING: ☆ ☆ ☆ ☆ ☆   **WILL I RETURN?** YES / NO

LODGING: **WHO I WENT WITH:**

THINGS TO DO: CAMP, BACKPACK

POPULAR ATTRACTIONS:

- Terlingua Ghost Town.
- Big Bend Ranch State Park.
- Big Bend National Park.
- Fort Leaton State Historic Site.
- Lajitas on the Rio Grande.

NOTES:

PASSPORT STAMPS

BASTROP STATE PARK

COUNTY: BASTROP   **ESTABLISHED:** 1937   **AREA (AC/HA):** 6,600 / 2,700

DATE(S) VISITED: SPRING ☐   SUMMER ☐   FALL ☐   WINTER ☐

WEATHER: ☀️☐ ☁️☐ 🌧️☐ ❄️☐ 🌦️☐ 🌬️☐   **TEMP.:**

FEE(S):   RATING: ☆ ☆ ☆ ☆ ☆   **WILL I RETURN?**   YES / NO

LODGING: **WHO I WENT WITH:**

THINGS TO DO: CAMP, HIKE, SWIM, BIKE, FISH, GEOCACHE

POPULAR ATTRACTIONS:

- Visitor's Center Museum.
- Lost Pines Art Center.
- Opera House.
- Zip Lining.
- Sugar Shack.

NOTES:

PASSPORT STAMPS

BATTLESHIP TEXAS STATE HISTORIC SITE

COUNTY: HARRIS   **ESTABLISHED:** 1948   **AREA (AC/HA):** - / -

DATE(S) VISITED: SPRING ☐   SUMMER ☐   FALL ☐   WINTER ☐

WEATHER: ☀☐ ⛅☐ 🌦☐ ❄☐ 🌧☐ 🌬☐   **TEMP.:**

FEE(S):   **RATING:** ☆ ☆ ☆ ☆ ☆   **WILL I RETURN?**   YES / NO

LODGING: **WHO I WENT WITH:**

THINGS TO DO: PICNIC

POPULAR ATTRACTIONS:

- More than 36,000 items are part of the Battleship Texas artifact collection.
- Recreational and educational experiences for visitors of all ages.
- Walk along the marsh trail to view the native prairie, tidal marsh and bottomland forest.

NOTES:

PASSPORT STAMPS

BENTSEN-RIO GRANDE VALLEY STATE PARK

COUNTY: HIDALGO   **ESTABLISHED:** 1944   **AREA (AC/HA):** 764 / 309

DATE(S) VISITED: SPRING ☐   SUMMER ☐   FALL ☐   WINTER ☐

WEATHER: ☀ ☐ ⛅ ☐ 🌧 ☐ ❄ ☐ 🌧 ☐ 🌬 ☐   **TEMP.:**

FEE(S):   RATING: ☆ ☆ ☆ ☆ ☆   **WILL I RETURN?**   YES / NO

LODGING: **WHO I WENT WITH:**

THINGS TO DO: BIRD WATCH, BUTTERFLY WATCH, HIKE, TRAM, BIKE, CAMP

POPULAR ATTRACTIONS:

- A two-story observation tower.
- Citizen science projects such as Hawk Watch and the Christmas Bird Count.

NOTES:

PASSPORT STAMPS

BIG BEND RANCH STATE PARK

COUNTY: PRESIDIO, BREWSTER   **ESTABLISHED:** 1988   **AREA (AC/HA):** 311,000 / 125,857

DATE(S) VISITED: SPRING ☐   SUMMER ☐   FALL ☐   WINTER ☐

WEATHER: ☀ ☐   ☁ ☐   🌧 ☐   ❄ ☐   ⛈ ☐   🌫 ☐   **TEMP.:**

FEE(S):   RATING: ☆ ☆ ☆ ☆ ☆   **WILL I RETURN?** YES / NO

LODGING: **WHO I WENT WITH:**

THINGS TO DO: HIKE, MOUNTAIN-BIKE, BACKPACK, PADDLE, RIDE HORSES

POPULAR ATTRACTIONS:

- Chihuahuan Desert Nature Center.
- McDonald Observatory.
- Fort Davis National Historic Site.
- Davis Mountains State Park.

NOTES:

PASSPORT STAMPS

BIG SPRING STATE PARK

COUNTY: HOWARD   **ESTABLISHED:** 1936   **AREA (AC/HA):** 382 / 154

DATE(S) VISITED: SPRING ☐   SUMMER ☐   FALL ☐   WINTER ☐

WEATHER: ☀ ☐   ⛅ ☐   🌧 ☐   ❄ ☐   🌦 ☐   🌬 ☐   **TEMP.:**

FEE(S):   **RATING:** ☆ ☆ ☆ ☆ ☆   **WILL I RETURN?**   YES / NO

LODGING: **WHO I WENT WITH:**

THINGS TO DO: PICNIC, NATURE STUDY, SIGHTSEEING

POPULAR ATTRACTIONS:

- Lake Colorado City State Park.
- Comanche Trail Park and Historical Spring.
- Moss Creek Lake.
- Heritage Museum/Potton House.
- One Mile Lake (Sandhill Crane Sanctuary - Observation Area).
- Unique 18-hole golf course.

NOTES:

PASSPORT STAMPS

BLANCO STATE PARK

COUNTY: BLANCO   **ESTABLISHED:** 1934   **AREA (AC/HA):** 105 / 42

DATE(S) VISITED: SPRING ☐   SUMMER ☐   FALL ☐   WINTER ☐

WEATHER: ☀☐ ⛅☐ 🌦☐ ❄☐ 🌧☐ 🌫☐   **TEMP.:**

FEE(S):   **RATING:** ☆ ☆ ☆ ☆ ☆   **WILL I RETURN?** YES / NO

LODGING: **WHO I WENT WITH:**

THINGS TO DO: FISH, SWIM, BOAT, PICNIC, PADDLE, CAMP, HIKE, GEOCACHE

POPULAR ATTRACTIONS:

- Sauer-Beckmann living history farm.
- Hill Country Science Mill.
- Lyndon B. Johnson State Park & Historic Site.

NOTES:

PASSPORT STAMPS

BONHAM STATE PARK

COUNTY: FANNIN   **ESTABLISHED:** 1933   **AREA (AC/HA):** 261 / 106

DATE(S) VISITED: SPRING ☐   SUMMER ☐   FALL ☐   WINTER ☐

WEATHER: ☀☐ ⛅☐ 🌧☐ ❄☐ ⛈☐ 🌬☐   **TEMP.:**

FEE(S):   RATING: ☆ ☆ ☆ ☆ ☆   **WILL I RETURN?** YES / NO

LODGING: **WHO I WENT WITH:**

THINGS TO DO: FISH, SWIM, BIKE, CAMP, HIKE, GEOCACHE

POPULAR ATTRACTIONS:

- Sam Bell Maxey House.
- Eisenhower Birthplace.

NOTES:

PASSPORT STAMPS

BRAZOS BEND STATE PARK

COUNTY: FORT BEND   **ESTABLISHED:** 1984   **AREA (AC/HA):** 4,897 / 1,982

DATE(S) VISITED: SPRING ☐   SUMMER ☐   FALL ☐   WINTER ☐

WEATHER: ☼ ☐   ⛅ ☐   🌧 ☐   ❄ ☐   🌦 ☐   🌬 ☐   **TEMP.:**

FEE(S):   RATING: ☆ ☆ ☆ ☆ ☆   **WILL I RETURN?** YES / NO

LODGING: **WHO I WENT WITH:**

THINGS TO DO: HIKE, BIKE, FISH, PICNIC, GEOCACHE, RIDE HORSES

POPULAR ATTRACTIONS:

- Varner-Hogg Plantation State Historic Site.
- George Ranch Historical Park.
- Sea Center Texas.

NOTES:

PASSPORT STAMPS

BUESCHER STATE PARK

COUNTY: BASTROP   **ESTABLISHED:** 1940   **AREA (AC/HA):** 1,017 / 411

DATE(S) VISITED: SPRING ☐   SUMMER ☐   FALL ☐   WINTER ☐

WEATHER: ☀☐ ⛅☐ ☁☐ ❄☐ 🌧☐ 🌬☐   **TEMP.:**

FEE(S):   **RATING:** ☆ ☆ ☆ ☆ ☆   **WILL I RETURN?** YES / NO

LODGING: **WHO I WENT WITH:**

THINGS TO DO: HIKE, BIKE, FISH, PADDLE, GEOCACHE

POPULAR ATTRACTIONS:

- 7.7-mile round trip hiking trail through the park's undeveloped area.
- Over 250 species of birds.

NOTES:

PASSPORT STAMPS

CADDO LAKE STATE PARK

COUNTY: HARRISON   **ESTABLISHED:** 1933   **AREA (AC/HA):** 468 / 189

DATE(S) VISITED: SPRING ☐   SUMMER ☐   FALL ☐   WINTER ☐

WEATHER: ☀ ☐ ⛅ ☐ 🌧 ☐ ❄ ☐ 🌦 ☐ 🌬 ☐   **TEMP.:**

FEE(S):   **RATING:** ☆ ☆ ☆ ☆ ☆   **WILL I RETURN?** YES / NO

LODGING: **WHO I WENT WITH:**

THINGS TO DO: FISH, PADDLE, HIKE, PICNIC, CAMP, GEOCACHE, BOAT

POPULAR ATTRACTIONS:

- Marshall, home of the Starr Family State Historic Site.
- Karnack, childhood home of Lady Bird Johnson.
- Jefferson, once the largest inland port in Texas.

NOTES:

PASSPORT STAMPS

CAPROCK CANYONS STATE PARK & TRAILWAY

COUNTY: BRISCOE   **ESTABLISHED:** 1982   **AREA (AC/HA):** 15,314 / 6,197

DATE(S) VISITED: SPRING ☐   SUMMER ☐   FALL ☐   WINTER ☐

WEATHER: ☀ ☐   ⛅ ☐   🌧 ☐   ❄ ☐   🌦 ☐   🌬 ☐   **TEMP.:**

FEE(S):   RATING: ☆ ☆ ☆ ☆ ☆   **WILL I RETURN?** YES / NO

LODGING: **WHO I WENT WITH:**

THINGS TO DO: HIKE, BIKE, RIDE HORSES, CAMP, GEOCACHE, PICNIC, BISON AND BATS WATCH

POPULAR ATTRACTIONS:

- Lake Meredith National Recreation Area.
- Greenbelt Reservoir.
- Mackenzie Reservoir.
- White River Reservoir.
- Bison Fest.

NOTES:

PASSPORT STAMPS

CEDAR HILL STATE PARK

COUNTY: DALLAS   **ESTABLISHED:** 1982   **AREA (AC/HA):** 1,826 / 739

DATE(S) VISITED: SPRING ☐   SUMMER ☐   FALL ☐   WINTER ☐

WEATHER: ☀ ☐ ⛅ ☐ 🌧 ☐ ❄ ☐ 🌧 ☐ 🌬 ☐   **TEMP.:**

FEE(S):   RATING: ☆ ☆ ☆ ☆ ☆   **WILL I RETURN?** YES / NO

LODGING: **WHO I WENT WITH:**

THINGS TO DO: HIKE, BIKE, PICNIC, CAMP, GEOCACHE, SWIM, FISH

POPULAR ATTRACTIONS:
- City of Cedar Hill.
- Downtown Fort Worth.
- Cedar Hill Museum of History.
- Cedar Mountain Nature Preserve.
- Dogwood Canyon Audubon Center.
- Hillside Village.
- International Museum of Cultures.
- Joe Pool Lake.
- Penn Farm Agricultural History Center.

NOTES:

PASSPORT STAMPS

CHOKE CANYON STATE PARK

COUNTY: LIVE OAK, MCMULLEN   **ESTABLISHED:** 1987   **AREA (AC/HA):** 25,670 / 10,390

DATE(S) VISITED: SPRING ☐   SUMMER ☐   FALL ☐   WINTER ☐

WEATHER: ☀ ☐   ⛅ ☐   🌧 ☐   ❄ ☐   ⛈ ☐   🌫 ☐   **TEMP.:**

FEE(S):   RATING: ☆ ☆ ☆ ☆ ☆   **WILL I RETURN?** YES / NO

LODGING: **WHO I WENT WITH:**

THINGS TO DO: FISH, BIRD WATCH, SWIM, CAMP, HIKE, GEOCACHE, BASKETBALL, TENNIS, SOCCER

POPULAR ATTRACTIONS:

- Large variety of birds and other wildlife as well as the great fishing.

NOTES:

PASSPORT STAMPS

CLEBURNE STATE PARK

COUNTY: JOHNSON   **ESTABLISHED:** 1938   **AREA (AC/HA):** 528 / 214

DATE(S) VISITED: SPRING ☐   SUMMER ☐   FALL ☐   WINTER ☐

WEATHER: ☀☐ ⛅☐ 🌧☐ ❄☐ ⛈☐ 🌬☐   **TEMP.:**

FEE(S):   **RATING:** ☆ ☆ ☆ ☆ ☆   **WILL I RETURN?** YES / NO

LODGING: **WHO I WENT WITH:**

THINGS TO DO: HIKE, FISH, SWIM, BOAT, CAMP, GEOCACHE, BIKE, CANOE, KAYAK

POPULAR ATTRACTIONS:

- Fossil Rim Wildlife Center in Glen Rose.
- Cleburne Carnegie Players.
- The Depot at Cleburne Station.
- Layland Museum of History.
- Plaza Theatre Company.
- The Chisholm Trail Outdoor Museum.

NOTES:

PASSPORT STAMPS

COLORADO BEND STATE PARK

COUNTY: LAMPASAS, SAN SABA   **ESTABLISHED:** 1987   **AREA (AC/HA):** 5,328 / 2,156

DATE(S) VISITED: SPRING ☐ SUMMER ☐ FALL ☐ WINTER ☐

WEATHER: ☀☐ ⛅☐ 🌧☐ ❄☐ ⛈☐ 🌬☐   **TEMP.:**

FEE(S):   RATING: ☆ ☆ ☆ ☆ ☆   **WILL I RETURN?** YES / NO

LODGING: **WHO I WENT WITH:**

THINGS TO DO: FISH, HIKE, BIKE, CAMP

POPULAR ATTRACTIONS:

- The Spicewood Springs trail.
- The Gorman Creek trail.

NOTES:

PASSPORT STAMPS

COOPER LAKE STATE PARK

COUNTY: COOPER   **ESTABLISHED:** 1992   **AREA (AC/HA):** 3,026 / 1,225

DATE(S) VISITED: SPRING ☐   SUMMER ☐   FALL ☐   WINTER ☐

WEATHER: ☀ ☐ ⛅ ☐ 🌧 ☐ ❄ ☐ ⛈ ☐ 🌬 ☐   **TEMP.:**

FEE(S):   RATING: ☆ ☆ ☆ ☆ ☆   **WILL I RETURN?** YES / NO

LODGING: **WHO I WENT WITH:**

THINGS TO DO: FISH, PICNIC, SWIM, BOAT, PADDLE, WATER-SKI, HIKE, BIKE, BIRD WATCH

POPULAR ATTRACTIONS:

- Southwest Dairy Center and Museum.
- Sam Bell Maxey House.
- Hopkins County Veterans Memorial.
- Coleman Park.

NOTES:

PASSPORT STAMPS

COPPER BREAKS STATE PARK

COUNTY: HARDEMAN   **ESTABLISHED:** 1974   **AREA (AC/HA):** 1,899 / 768

DATE(S) VISITED: SPRING ☐ SUMMER ☐ FALL ☐ WINTER ☐

WEATHER: ☀ ☐ ⛅ ☐ 🌦 ☐ ❄ ☐ ⛈ ☐ 🌫 ☐ **TEMP.:**

FEE(S):   RATING: ☆ ☆ ☆ ☆ ☆   **WILL I RETURN?** YES / NO

LODGING: **WHO I WENT WITH:**

THINGS TO DO: HIKE, BIKE, FISH, SWIM, CAMP, STARGAZE, PADDLE, BOAT

POPULAR ATTRACTIONS:

- Short Bull Canyon Trail.
- Long Bull Canyon Loop.
- Rocky Ledges Loop.

NOTES:

PASSPORT STAMPS

DAINGERFIELD STATE PARK

COUNTY: MORRIS   **ESTABLISHED:** 1938   **AREA (AC/HA):** 507 / 205

DATE(S) VISITED: SPRING ☐   SUMMER ☐   FALL ☐   WINTER ☐

WEATHER: ☀ ☐ ⛅ ☐ 🌧 ☐ ❄ ☐ ⛈ ☐ 🌬 ☐   **TEMP.:**

FEE(S):   RATING: ☆ ☆ ☆ ☆ ☆   **WILL I RETURN?** YES / NO

LODGING: **WHO I WENT WITH:**

THINGS TO DO: GEOCACHE, HIKE, BIRD WATCH, CAMP, PICNIC, SWIM, BOAT, PADDLE, FISH

POPULAR ATTRACTIONS:

- The pre-Civil War town of Jefferson.
- Morris Theatre.
- The Greer Farm.
- Lake O' The Pines.
- Wright Patman Lake.

NOTES:

PASSPORT STAMPS

DAVIS MOUNTAINS STATE PARK

COUNTY: DAVIS   **ESTABLISHED:** 1938   **AREA (AC/HA):** 2,709 / 1,096

DATE(S) VISITED: SPRING ☐ SUMMER ☐ FALL ☐ WINTER ☐

WEATHER: ☀☐ ⛅☐ 🌧☐ ❄☐ 🌧☐ 🌫☐ **TEMP.:**

FEE(S):   RATING: ☆ ☆ ☆ ☆ ☆   **WILL I RETURN?** YES / NO

LODGING: **WHO I WENT WITH:**

THINGS TO DO: HIKE, BACKPACK, BIKE, CAMP, STARGAZE, GEOCACHE

POPULAR ATTRACTIONS:

- Fort Davis National Historic Site.
- McDonald Observatory.
- Chihuahuan Desert Nature Center.
- Scenic Loop Drive.
- Davis Mountains Preserve.
- Museum of the Big Bend in Alpine.

NOTES:

PASSPORT STAMPS

DEVILS RIVER STATE NATURAL AREA

COUNTY: VAL VERDE   **ESTABLISHED:** 1988   **AREA (AC/HA):** 37,000 / 15,000

DATE(S) VISITED: SPRING ☐   SUMMER ☐   FALL ☐   WINTER ☐

WEATHER: ☀☐ ⛅☐ 🌦☐ ❄☐ 🌧☐ 🌬☐   **TEMP.:**

FEE(S):   RATING: ☆ ☆ ☆ ☆ ☆   **WILL I RETURN?**   YES / NO

LODGING: **WHO I WENT WITH:**

THINGS TO DO: SWIM, FISH, PADDLE, BIKE, HIKE

POPULAR ATTRACTIONS:

- Pictographs painted with red panthers which archeologists have dated to 3000 b.c.
- Wildlife such as snakes, foxes, armadillos, porcupines, skunks, raccoons, and more occasionally bobcats, mountain lions, and the rare black bear that wanders up from Mexico.

NOTES:

PASSPORT STAMPS

DEVIL'S SINKHOLE STATE NATURAL AREA

COUNTY: EDWARDS   **ESTABLISHED:** 1985   **AREA (AC/HA):** 1,859 / 752

DATE(S) VISITED: SPRING ☐ SUMMER ☐ FALL ☐ WINTER ☐

WEATHER: ☀ ☐ ⛅ ☐ 🌧 ☐ ❄ ☐ 🌧 ☐ 🌬 ☐   **TEMP.:**

FEE(S):   RATING: ☆ ☆ ☆ ☆ ☆   **WILL I RETURN?** YES / NO

LODGING: **WHO I WENT WITH:**

THINGS TO DO: HIKE, BATS WATCH

POPULAR ATTRACTIONS:

- Evening bat flight tours.
- Kickapoo Cavern State Park.

NOTES:

PASSPORT STAMPS

DINOSAUR VALLEY STATE PARK

COUNTY: SOMERVELL   **ESTABLISHED:** 1972   **AREA (AC/HA):** 1,524 / 617

DATE(S) VISITED: SPRING ☐   SUMMER ☐   FALL ☐   WINTER ☐

WEATHER: ☀ ☐   ☁ ☐   🌧 ☐   ❄ ☐   ⛈ ☐   🌫 ☐   **TEMP.:**

FEE(S):   RATING: ☆ ☆ ☆ ☆ ☆   **WILL I RETURN?** YES / NO

LODGING: **WHO I WENT WITH:**

THINGS TO DO: CAMP, PICNIC, HIKE, BIKE, SWIM, FISH, PADDLE, GEOCACHE

POPULAR ATTRACTIONS:

- Glen Rose, the "Dinosaur Capital of Texas": Tour the square, visit Barnard's Mill and Art Museum and the Somervell County Museum.
- Fossil Rim Wildlife Center.
- Acton State Historic Site.
- Comanche Peak Visitors Center.

NOTES:

PASSPORT STAMPS

EISENHOWER STATE PARK

COUNTY: GRAYSON   **ESTABLISHED:** 1954   **AREA (AC/HA):** 463 / 187

DATE(S) VISITED: SPRING ☐ SUMMER ☐ FALL ☐ WINTER ☐

WEATHER: ☀ ☐ ⛅ ☐ 🌧 ☐ ❄ ☐ ⛈ ☐ 🌬 ☐   **TEMP.:**

FEE(S):   RATING: ☆ ☆ ☆ ☆ ☆   **WILL I RETURN?** YES / NO

LODGING: **WHO I WENT WITH:**

THINGS TO DO: BIKE, SWIM, PICNIC, FISH, CAMP

POPULAR ATTRACTIONS:

- Red River Railroad Museum.
- Grayson County Frontier Village.

NOTES:

PASSPORT STAMPS

ENCHANTED ROCK STATE NATURAL AREA

COUNTY: LLANO   **ESTABLISHED:** 1978   **AREA (AC/HA):** 1,640 / 663

DATE(S) VISITED: SPRING ☐   SUMMER ☐   FALL ☐   WINTER ☐

WEATHER: ☀ ☐   ⛅ ☐   🌧 ☐   ❄ ☐   ⛈ ☐   🌬 ☐   **TEMP.:**

FEE(S):   **RATING:** ☆ ☆ ☆ ☆ ☆   **WILL I RETURN?** YES / NO

LODGING: **WHO I WENT WITH:**

THINGS TO DO: HIKE, BACKPACK, CAMP, PICNIC, GEOCACHE, STARGAZE

POPULAR ATTRACTIONS:

- Fredericksburg.
- Deer Capital of Texas.
- Sauer-Beckmann living history farm.
- Lyndon B. Johnson National Historical Park.

NOTES:

PASSPORT STAMPS

ESTERO LLANO GRANDE STATE PARK

COUNTY: HIDALGO   **ESTABLISHED:** 2006   **AREA (AC/HA):** 230 / 93

DATE(S) VISITED: SPRING ☐   SUMMER ☐   FALL ☐   WINTER ☐

WEATHER: ☀☐ ⛅☐ 🌧☐ ❄☐ ⛈☐ 🌬☐   **TEMP.:**

FEE(S):   RATING: ☆ ☆ ☆ ☆ ☆   **WILL I RETURN?** YES / NO

LODGING: **WHO I WENT WITH:**

THINGS TO DO: BIRD WATCH, GEOCACHE, BIKE

POPULAR ATTRACTIONS:

- Alligator Lake.

NOTES:

PASSPORT STAMPS

FAIRFIELD LAKE STATE PARK

COUNTY: FREESTONE   **ESTABLISHED:** 1976   **AREA (AC/HA):** 1,460 / 591

DATE(S) VISITED: SPRING ☐   SUMMER ☐   FALL ☐   WINTER ☐

WEATHER: ☀ ☐ ⛅ ☐ 🌧 ☐ ❄ ☐ ⛈ ☐ 🌬 ☐   **TEMP.:**

FEE(S):   RATING: ☆ ☆ ☆ ☆ ☆   **WILL I RETURN?** YES / NO

LODGING: **WHO I WENT WITH:**

THINGS TO DO: CAMP, BACKPACK, HIKE, BIRD WATCH, FISH, PADDLE, SWIM

POPULAR ATTRACTIONS:

- Texas State Railroad.
- Fort Parker State Park.
- Old Fort Parker.
- Confederate Reunion Grounds State Historic Site.
- Stewards Mill.
- B-RI Railroad Museum in Teague.
- Freestone County Museum.
- Texas Freshwater Fisheries Center in Athens.

NOTES:

PASSPORT STAMPS

FALCON STATE PARK

COUNTY: ZAPATA, STARR   **ESTABLISHED:** 1965   **AREA (AC/HA):** 83,654 / 33,854

DATE(S) VISITED: SPRING ☐   SUMMER ☐   FALL ☐   WINTER ☐

WEATHER: ☀☐ ⛅☐ ☁☐ ❄☐ 🌧☐ 🌬☐   **TEMP.:**

FEE(S):   **RATING:** ☆ ☆ ☆ ☆ ☆   **WILL I RETURN?** YES / NO

LODGING: **WHO I WENT WITH:**

THINGS TO DO: FISH, SWIM, CAMP, BIRD WATCH, WATER SKI, BOAT, GEOCACHE, HIKE

POPULAR ATTRACTIONS:

- Roma Historic District.
- World Birding Center: Roma Bluffs.
- Roma Historical Museum.
- Fort Ringgold in Rio Grande City.
- Texas Tropical Trail Region.

NOTES:

PASSPORT STAMPS

FORT BOGGY STATE PARK

COUNTY: LEON   **ESTABLISHED:** 1985   **AREA (AC/HA):** 1,847 / 747

DATE(S) VISITED: SPRING ☐   SUMMER ☐   FALL ☐   WINTER ☐

WEATHER: ☀ ☐   ⛅ ☐   🌧 ☐   ❄ ☐   ⛈ ☐   🌫 ☐   **TEMP.:**

FEE(S):   **RATING:** ☆ ☆ ☆ ☆ ☆   **WILL I RETURN?** YES / NO

LODGING: **WHO I WENT WITH:**

THINGS TO DO: HIKE, BIKE, GEOCACHE, SWIM, FISH, PADDLE

POPULAR ATTRACTIONS:

- Texas State Railroad.
- Confederate Reunion Grounds State Historic Site.
- Nearby cities include Rusk, Palestine and Fairfield.
- Freestone County Historical Museum.

NOTES:

PASSPORT STAMPS

FORT LEATON STATE HISTORIC SITE

COUNTY: PRESIDIO   **ESTABLISHED:** 1973   **AREA (AC/HA):** 24 / 9

DATE(S) VISITED: SPRING ☐   SUMMER ☐   FALL ☐   WINTER ☐

WEATHER: ☀ ☐   ⛅ ☐   🌧 ☐   ❄ ☐   ⛈ ☐   🌫 ☐   **TEMP.:**

FEE(S):   RATING: ☆ ☆ ☆ ☆ ☆   **WILL I RETURN?**   YES / NO

LODGING: **WHO I WENT WITH:**

THINGS TO DO: PICNIC, BACKPACK, CAMP

POPULAR ATTRACTIONS:

- Big Bend Ranch State Park.
- Davis Mountains State Park.
- Barton Warnock Visitor Center.
- Big Bend National Park.
- Presidio.
- Ojinaga.
- Chihuahua.
- Mexico (gateway to Copper Canyon).

NOTES:

PASSPORT STAMPS

FORT PARKER STATE PARK

COUNTY: LIMESTONE   **ESTABLISHED:** 1941   **AREA (AC/HA):** 1,458 / 590

DATE(S) VISITED: SPRING ☐   SUMMER ☐   FALL ☐   WINTER ☐

WEATHER: ☀ ☐   ⛅ ☐   🌧 ☐   ❄ ☐   ⛈ ☐   🌬 ☐   **TEMP.:**

FEE(S):   RATING: ☆ ☆ ☆ ☆ ☆   **WILL I RETURN?** YES / NO

LODGING: **WHO I WENT WITH:**

THINGS TO DO: SWIM, FISH, BIKE, CAMP, PICNIC, BIRD WATCH, PADDLE, GEOCACHE

POPULAR ATTRACTIONS:

- Old Fort Parker.
- Confederate Reunion Grounds State Historic Site.

NOTES:

PASSPORT STAMPS

FORT RICHARDSON STATE PARK, HISTORIC SITE & LOST CREEK RESERVOIR STATE TRAILWAY

COUNTY: JACK   **ESTABLISHED:** 1968   **AREA (AC/HA):** 454 / 183

DATE(S) VISITED: SPRING ☐   SUMMER ☐   FALL ☐   WINTER ☐

WEATHER: ☀ ☐ ⛅ ☐ 🌧 ☐ ❄ ☐ 🌧 ☐ 🌬 ☐   **TEMP.:**

FEE(S):   **RATING:** ☆ ☆ ☆ ☆ ☆   **WILL I RETURN?** YES / NO

LODGING: **WHO I WENT WITH:**

THINGS TO DO: CAMP, HIKE, BIKE, FISH, SWIM, PADDLE, GEOCACHE

POPULAR ATTRACTIONS:

- Lost Creek Reservoir State Trailway.

NOTES:

PASSPORT STAMPS

FRANKLIN MOUNTAINS STATE PARK

COUNTY: EL PASO   **ESTABLISHED:** 1987   **AREA (AC/HA):** 24,247 / 9,812

DATE(S) VISITED: SPRING ☐   SUMMER ☐   FALL ☐   WINTER ☐

WEATHER: ☀ ☐ ⛅ ☐ 🌧 ☐ ❄ ☐ 🌧 ☐ 🌬 ☐   **TEMP.:**

FEE(S):   **RATING:** ☆ ☆ ☆ ☆ ☆   **WILL I RETURN?** YES / NO

LODGING: **WHO I WENT WITH:**

THINGS TO DO: HIKE, CAMP, ROCK, MOUNTAIN BIKE

POPULAR ATTRACTIONS:

- Wilderness Park Museum.
- Chamizal National Memorial.
- Ciudad Juarez, Mexico.

NOTES:

PASSPORT STAMPS

GALVESTON ISLAND STATE PARK

COUNTY: GALVESTON   **ESTABLISHED:** 1975   **AREA (AC/HA):** 2,013 / 814

DATE(S) VISITED: SPRING ☐ SUMMER ☐ FALL ☐ WINTER ☐

WEATHER: ☼ ☐ ☁ ☐ 🌧 ☐ ❄ ☐ 🌧 ☐ 🌬 ☐   **TEMP.:**

FEE(S):   **RATING:** ☆ ☆ ☆ ☆ ☆   **WILL I RETURN?** YES / NO

LODGING: **WHO I WENT WITH:**

THINGS TO DO: SWIM, FISH, PICNIC, BIRD WATCH, MOUNTAIN BIKE, PADDLE, CAMP, GEOCACHE

POPULAR ATTRACTIONS:

- Galveston.
- Moody Gardens.

NOTES:

PASSPORT STAMPS

GARNER STATE PARK

COUNTY: UVALDE   **ESTABLISHED:** 1941   **AREA (AC/HA):** 1,420 / 570

DATE(S) VISITED: SPRING ☐   SUMMER ☐   FALL ☐   WINTER ☐

WEATHER: ☀☐ ⛅☐ 🌦☐ ❄☐ ⛈☐ 🌬☐   **TEMP.:**

FEE(S):   RATING: ☆ ☆ ☆ ☆ ☆   **WILL I RETURN?** YES / NO

LODGING: **WHO I WENT WITH:**

THINGS TO DO: SWIM, HIKE, CAMP, PICNIC, CANOE, FISH, MINI GOLF, BIKE, GEOCACHE

POPULAR ATTRACTIONS:

- Briscoe-Garner Museum.
- Fort Inge.
- Texas Ranger Camp.
- Frio Bat Flight.

NOTES:

PASSPORT STAMPS

GOLIAD STATE PARK & HISTORIC SITE

COUNTY: GOLIAD   **ESTABLISHED:** 1936   **AREA (AC/HA):** 188 / 76

DATE(S) VISITED: SPRING ☐   SUMMER ☐   FALL ☐   WINTER ☐

WEATHER: ☀ ☐ ☁ ☐ 🌧 ☐ ❄ ☐ ⛈ ☐ 🌬 ☐   **TEMP.:**

FEE(S):   RATING: ☆ ☆ ☆ ☆ ☆   **WILL I RETURN?** YES / NO

LODGING: **WHO I WENT WITH:**

THINGS TO DO: HIKE, BIKE, CAMP, PICNIC, FISH, PADDLE

POPULAR ATTRACTIONS:

- Goliad area historic sites.
- Goliad County Courthouse.

NOTES:

PASSPORT STAMPS

GOOSE ISLAND STATE PARK

COUNTY: ARANSAS   **ESTABLISHED:** 1935   **AREA (AC/HA):** 321 / 130

DATE(S) VISITED: SPRING ☐   SUMMER ☐   FALL ☐   WINTER ☐

WEATHER: ☀ ☐   ⛅ ☐   🌧 ☐   ❄ ☐   ⛈ ☐   🌬 ☐   **TEMP.:**

FEE(S):   **RATING:** ☆ ☆ ☆ ☆ ☆   **WILL I RETURN?**   YES / NO

LODGING: **WHO I WENT WITH:**

THINGS TO DO: CAMP, FISH, HIKE, GEOCACHE, BOAT

POPULAR ATTRACTIONS:

- Aransas National Wildlife Refuge.
- Texas Maritime Museum.
- Fulton Mansion State Historic Site.
- Rockport Beach.
- Texas State Aquarium.
- U.S.S. Lexington.

NOTES:

PASSPORT STAMPS

GOVERNMENT CANYON STATE NATURAL AREA

COUNTY: BEXAR   **ESTABLISHED:** 1993   **AREA (AC/HA):** 12,085 / 4,891

DATE(S) VISITED: SPRING ☐   SUMMER ☐   FALL ☐   WINTER ☐

WEATHER: ☀ ☐ ☁ ☐ 🌧 ☐ ❄ ☐ 🌧 ☐ 🌫 ☐   **TEMP.:**

FEE(S):   RATING: ☆ ☆ ☆ ☆ ☆   **WILL I RETURN?** YES / NO

LODGING: **WHO I WENT WITH:**

THINGS TO DO: CAMP, HIKE, BIKE, PICNIC, GEOCACHE, BIRD WATCH

POPULAR ATTRACTIONS:

- The Alamo.
- San Antonio Missions National Historical Park.
- Casa Navarro State Historic Site.
- Sea World.
- Fiesta Texas.
- Landmark Inn State Historic Site.

NOTES:

PASSPORT STAMPS

GUADALUPE RIVER STATE PARK

COUNTY: COMALL, KENDALL   **ESTABLISHED:** 1983   **AREA (AC/HA):** 1,938 / 785

DATE(S) VISITED: SPRING ☐   SUMMER ☐   FALL ☐   WINTER ☐

WEATHER: ☀ ☐   ⛅ ☐   🌧 ☐   ❄ ☐   ⛈ ☐   🌫 ☐   **TEMP.:**

FEE(S):   RATING: ☆ ☆ ☆ ☆ ☆   **WILL I RETURN?** YES / NO

LODGING: **WHO I WENT WITH:**

THINGS TO DO: SWIM, FISH, CANOE, CAMP, HIKE, MOUNTAIN BIKE, PICNIC, GEOCACHE, PADDLE

POPULAR ATTRACTIONS:

- Boern.
- New Braunfels.
- Paddle the Upper Guadalupe – Nichol's Landing Paddling Trail.
- San Antonio (30 miles away) offers history, nature, museums, shopping and more.

NOTES:

PASSPORT STAMPS

HILL COUNTRY STATE NATURAL AREA

COUNTY: BANDERA, MEDINA   **ESTABLISHED:** 1984   **AREA (AC/HA):** 5,369 / 2,173

DATE(S) VISITED: SPRING ☐ SUMMER ☐ FALL ☐ WINTER ☐

WEATHER: ☀☐ ⛅☐ 🌧☐ ❄☐ 🌧☐ 🌬☐   **TEMP.:**

FEE(S):   RATING: ☆ ☆ ☆ ☆ ☆   **WILL I RETURN?** YES / NO

LODGING: **WHO I WENT WITH:**

THINGS TO DO: CAMP, BACKPACK, MOUNTAIN BIKE, HORSEBACK RIDE

POPULAR ATTRACTIONS:

- Dude ranches.
- Kayak/tube rentals on the Medina River.
- Rodeos and other special events in nearby Bandera, Medina and Pipe Creek.

NOTES:

PASSPORT STAMPS

HONEY CREEK STATE NATURAL AREA

COUNTY: COMAL   **ESTABLISHED:** 1985   **AREA (AC/HA):** 2,293 / 928

DATE(S) VISITED: SPRING ☐   SUMMER ☐   FALL ☐   WINTER ☐

WEATHER: ☀ ☐   ⛅ ☐   🌧 ☐   ❄ ☐   ⛈ ☐   🌬 ☐   **TEMP.:**

FEE(S):   RATING: ☆ ☆ ☆ ☆ ☆   **WILL I RETURN?** YES / NO

LODGING: **WHO I WENT WITH:**

THINGS TO DO: CAMP, HIKE, SWIM

POPULAR ATTRACTIONS:

- Rust House.

NOTES:

PASSPORT STAMPS

HUECO TANKS STATE PARK & HISTORIC SITE

COUNTY: EL PASO   **ESTABLISHED:** 1970   **AREA (AC/HA):** 860 / 350

DATE(S) VISITED: SPRING ☐   SUMMER ☐   FALL ☐   WINTER ☐

WEATHER: ☀ ☐   ⛅ ☐   🌧 ☐   ❄ ☐   ⛈ ☐   🌬 ☐   **TEMP.:**

FEE(S):   RATING: ☆ ☆ ☆ ☆ ☆   **WILL I RETURN?** YES / NO

LODGING: **WHO I WENT WITH:**

THINGS TO DO: HIKE, ROCK CLIMB, BIRD WATCH, PICNIC, STARGAZE

POPULAR ATTRACTIONS:

- Old Fort Bliss.
- Texas Mountain Trail Region.
- El Paso Uplands Loop, part of the Great Texas Wildlife Trails.

NOTES:

PASSPORT STAMPS

HUNTSVILLE STATE PARK

COUNTY: WALKER   **ESTABLISHED:** 1956   **AREA (AC/HA):** 2,083 / 843

DATE(S) VISITED: SPRING ☐   SUMMER ☐   FALL ☐   WINTER ☐

WEATHER: ☀️☐ ⛅☐ 🌦️☐ ❄️☐ 🌧️☐ 🌬️☐   **TEMP.:**

FEE(S):   **RATING:** ☆ ☆ ☆ ☆ ☆   **WILL I RETURN?** YES / NO

LODGING: **WHO I WENT WITH:**

THINGS TO DO: CAMP, HIKE, BIKE, PICNIC, FISH, SWIM, PADDLE, GEOCACHE

POPULAR ATTRACTIONS:

- Alligators in the park.
- Sam Houston Memorial Museum.
- Sam Houston Statue.
- Sam Houston National Forest.
- Lone Star Hiking Trail.

NOTES:

PASSPORT STAMPS

INDIAN LODGE

COUNTY: JEFF DAVIS   **ESTABLISHED:** 1939   **AREA (AC/HA):** - / -

DATE(S) VISITED: SPRING ☐ SUMMER ☐ FALL ☐ WINTER ☐

WEATHER: ☀☐ ☁☐ 🌧☐ ❄☐ ⛈☐ 🌬☐   **TEMP.:**

FEE(S):   RATING: ☆ ☆ ☆ ☆ ☆   **WILL I RETURN?** YES / NO

LODGING: **WHO I WENT WITH:**

THINGS TO DO: SWIM, HIKE, BIKE

POPULAR ATTRACTIONS:

- Fort Davis National Historic Site.
- McDonald Observatory.
- Chihuahuan Desert Nature Center.
- Scenic Loop Drive.
- Davis Mountains Preserve.
- Museum of the Big Bend in Alpine.

NOTES:

PASSPORT STAMPS

INKS LAKE STATE PARK

COUNTY: BURNET   **ESTABLISHED:** 1950   **AREA (AC/HA):** 1,201 / 486

DATE(S) VISITED: SPRING ☐   SUMMER ☐   FALL ☐   WINTER ☐

WEATHER: ☀ ☐   ⛅ ☐   🌧 ☐   ❄ ☐   🌧 ☐   🌬 ☐   **TEMP.:**

FEE(S):   **RATING:** ☆ ☆ ☆ ☆ ☆   **WILL I RETURN?** YES / NO

LODGING: **WHO I WENT WITH:**

THINGS TO DO: CAMP, BACKPACK, GEOCACHE, VOLLEYBALL, PICNIC, PADDLE, FISH

POPULAR ATTRACTIONS:

- Longhorn Cavern State Park.
- Inks Dam National Fish Hatchery.
- Buchanan Dam (the largest multiarch dam in the world).
- Vanishing Texas River Cruise.
- Balcones Canyonlands National Wildlife Refuge.

NOTES:

PASSPORT STAMPS

KICKAPOO CAVERN STATE PARK

COUNTY: KINNEY, EDWARDS   **ESTABLISHED:** 1991   **AREA (AC/HA):** 6,368 / 2,577

DATE(S) VISITED: SPRING ☐   SUMMER ☐   FALL ☐   WINTER ☐

WEATHER: ☀☐ ⛅☐ 🌧☐ ❄☐ ⛈☐ 🌬☐   **TEMP.:**

FEE(S):   **RATING:** ☆ ☆ ☆ ☆ ☆   **WILL I RETURN?**   YES / NO

LODGING: **WHO I WENT WITH:**

THINGS TO DO: HIKE, MOUNTAIN BIKE, CAMP, BIRD WATCH, GEOCACH

POPULAR ATTRACTIONS:

- Kickapoo Cavern.
- Stuart Bat Cave.

NOTES:

PASSPORT STAMPS

LAKE ARROWHEAD STATE PARK

COUNTY: CLAY   **ESTABLISHED:** 1970   **AREA (AC/HA):** 524 / 212

DATE(S) VISITED: SPRING ☐   SUMMER ☐   FALL ☐   WINTER ☐

WEATHER: ☀ ☐   ⛅ ☐   🌧 ☐   ❄ ☐   ⛈ ☐   🌫 ☐   **TEMP.:**

FEE(S):   **RATING:** ☆ ☆ ☆ ☆ ☆   **WILL I RETURN?** YES / NO

LODGING: **WHO I WENT WITH:**

THINGS TO DO: FISH, SWIM, WATER SKI, DISC GOLF, PICNIC, CAMP, HIKE, BOAT

POPULAR ATTRACTIONS:

- Fort Richardson State Park, Historic Site & Lost Creek Reservoir State Trailway.
- Possum Kingdom State Park.
- Copper Breaks State Park.
- Red River Rodeo (June).
- Texas/Oklahoma Jr. Golf Tour (June).
- Hotter 'N Hell Hundred Bicycle Ride (August).
- Midwestern State University.
- Sheppard Air Force Base.
- Wichita Mountains Wildlife Refuge.

NOTES:

PASSPORT STAMPS

LAKE BOB SANDLIN STATE PARK

COUNTY: TITUS, CAMP, FRANKLIN   **ESTABLISHED:** 1987   **AREA (AC/HA):** 641 / 259

DATE(S) VISITED: SPRING ☐   SUMMER ☐   FALL ☐   WINTER ☐

WEATHER: ☀ ☐ ⛅ ☐ 🌧 ☐ ❄ ☐ ⛈ ☐ 🌬 ☐   **TEMP.:**

FEE(S):   **RATING:** ☆ ☆ ☆ ☆ ☆   **WILL I RETURN?**   YES / NO

LODGING: **WHO I WENT WITH:**

THINGS TO DO: PICNIC, HIKE, CAMP, GEOCACHE, MOUNTAIN BIKE

POPULAR ATTRACTIONS:

- Mount Pleasant.
- Mount Vernon.
- Governor Hogg Shrine in Quitman.
- Lake Monticello.
- Lake Cypress Springs.
- Ezekiel Airship in Pittsburg.

NOTES:

PASSPORT STAMPS

LAKE BROWNWOOD STATE PARK

COUNTY: BROWN   **ESTABLISHED:** 1938   **AREA (AC/HA):** 537 / 218

DATE(S) VISITED: SPRING ☐   SUMMER ☐   FALL ☐   WINTER ☐

WEATHER: ☀☐ ⛅☐ 🌧☐ ❄☐ ⛈☐ 🌬☐   **TEMP.:**

FEE(S):   RATING: ☆ ☆ ☆ ☆ ☆   **WILL I RETURN?**   YES / NO

LODGING: **WHO I WENT WITH:**

THINGS TO DO: FISH, SWIM, WATER SKI, JET SKI, PADDLE, CAMP, BOAT, GEOCACHE

POPULAR ATTRACTIONS:

- Nopales Ridge Trail.

NOTES:

PASSPORT STAMPS

LAKE CASA BLANCA INTERNATIONAL STATE PARK

COUNTY: WEBB   **ESTABLISHED:** 1991   **AREA (AC/HA):** 525 / 212

DATE(S) VISITED: SPRING ☐   SUMMER ☐   FALL ☐   WINTER ☐

WEATHER: ☀ ☐ ⛅ ☐ 🌧 ☐ ❄ ☐ 🌧 ☐ 🌬 ☐   **TEMP.:**

FEE(S):   RATING: ☆ ☆ ☆ ☆ ☆   **WILL I RETURN?** YES / NO

LODGING: **WHO I WENT WITH:**

THINGS TO DO: SWIM, FISH, BOAT, WATER SKI, HIKE, BIKE, BIRD WATCH, GEOCACHE, CAMP

POPULAR ATTRACTIONS:

- Laredo city.

NOTES:

PASSPORT STAMPS

LAKE COLORADO CITY STATE PARK

COUNTY: MITCHELL   **ESTABLISHED:** 1972   **AREA (AC/HA):** 500 / 200

DATE(S) VISITED: SPRING ☐   SUMMER ☐   FALL ☐   WINTER ☐

WEATHER: ☀️☐ ⛅☐ 🌦️☐ ❄️☐ 🌧️☐ 🌫️☐   **TEMP.:**

FEE(S):   RATING: ☆ ☆ ☆ ☆ ☆   **WILL I RETURN?**   YES / NO

LODGING: **WHO I WENT WITH:**

THINGS TO DO: FISH, SWIM, PADDLE, CAMP, PICNIC, HIKE, GEOCACHE, KAYAK

POPULAR ATTRACTIONS:

- Colorado city.
- Abilene.
- Midland.

NOTES:

PASSPORT STAMPS

LAKE CORPUS CHRISTI STATE PARK

COUNTY: SAN PATRICIO   **ESTABLISHED:** 1934   **AREA (AC/HA):** 356 / 144

DATE(S) VISITED: SPRING ☐   SUMMER ☐   FALL ☐   WINTER ☐

WEATHER: ☀☐ ☁☐ 🌧☐ ❄☐ 🌧☐ 🌬☐   **TEMP.:**

FEE(S):   RATING: ☆ ☆ ☆ ☆ ☆   **WILL I RETURN?**   YES / NO

LODGING: **WHO I WENT WITH:**

THINGS TO DO: SWIM, PADDLE, FISH, BOAT, WATER SKI, CAMP, HIKE, BIKE, GEOCACHE

POPULAR ATTRACTIONS:

- Bayside town of Corpus Christi.

NOTES:

PASSPORT STAMPS

LAKE LIVINGSTON STATE PARK

COUNTY: POLK   **ESTABLISHED:** 1977   **AREA (AC/HA):** 635 / 257

DATE(S) VISITED: SPRING ☐ SUMMER ☐ FALL ☐ WINTER ☐

WEATHER: ☀︎ ☐ ⛅ ☐ 🌧 ☐ ❄ ☐ ⛈ ☐ 🌫 ☐   **TEMP.:**

FEE(S):   RATING: ☆ ☆ ☆ ☆ ☆   **WILL I RETURN?** YES / NO

LODGING: **WHO I WENT WITH:**

THINGS TO DO: SWIM, FISH, BOAT, HIKE, CAMP, PICNIC, GEOCACHE, MOUNTAIN BIKE

POPULAR ATTRACTIONS:

- Big Thicket National Preserve.
- Sam Houston National Forest.
- Polk County Library.
- Memorial Museum.

NOTES:

PASSPORT STAMPS

LAKE MINERAL WELLS STATE PARK & TRAILWAY

COUNTY: PARKER   **ESTABLISHED:** 1981   **AREA (AC/HA):** 3,282 / 1,328

DATE(S) VISITED: SPRING ☐   SUMMER ☐   FALL ☐   WINTER ☐

WEATHER: ☀☐ ⛅☐ 🌧☐ ❄☐ ⛈☐ 🌬☐   **TEMP.:**

FEE(S):   RATING: ☆ ☆ ☆ ☆ ☆   **WILL I RETURN?** YES / NO

LODGING: **WHO I WENT WITH:**

THINGS TO DO: SWIM, FISH, BOAT, HIKE, CAMP, GEOCACHE, BIKE, ROCK CLIMB

POPULAR ATTRACTIONS:

- Clark Gardens.
- Mineral Wells Fossil Park.
- Museum of the Americas.
- Chandor Gardens.

NOTES:

PASSPORT STAMPS

LAKE SOMERVILLE STATE PARK & TRAILWAY

COUNTY: BURLESON, LEE   **ESTABLISHED:** 1970   **AREA (AC/HA):** 5,520 / 2,233

DATE(S) VISITED: SPRING ☐   SUMMER ☐   FALL ☐   WINTER ☐

WEATHER: ☀ ☐   ⛅ ☐   🌧 ☐   ❄ ☐   🌧 ☐   🌬 ☐   **TEMP.:**

FEE(S):   **RATING:** ☆ ☆ ☆ ☆ ☆   **WILL I RETURN?** YES / NO

LODGING: **WHO I WENT WITH:**

THINGS TO DO: SWIM, FISH, BOAT, PADDLE, CAMP, PICNIC, HIKE, MOUNTAIN BIKE, GEOCACHE

POPULAR ATTRACTIONS:

- San Felipe State Historic Site.
- Bluebell Creamery.
- Texas A&M University.

NOTES:

PASSPORT STAMPS

LAKE TAWAKONI STATE PARK

COUNTY: HUNT   **ESTABLISHED:** 1984   **AREA (AC/HA):** 376 / 152

DATE(S) VISITED: SPRING ☐ SUMMER ☐ FALL ☐ WINTER ☐

WEATHER: ☀ ☐ ⛅ ☐ 🌧 ☐ ❄ ☐ 🌧 ☐ 🌬 ☐ **TEMP.:**

FEE(S):   RATING: ☆ ☆ ☆ ☆ ☆   **WILL I RETURN?** YES / NO

LODGING: **WHO I WENT WITH:**

THINGS TO DO: SWIM, FISH, BOAT, HIKE, MOUNTAIN BIKE, BIRD WATCH, CAMP, GEOCACHE

POPULAR ATTRACTIONS:

- Governor Hogg Shrine Historic Site in Quitman.
- First Monday Trade Days at Canton.

NOTES:

PASSPORT STAMPS

LAKE WHITNEY STATE PARK

COUNTY: HILL   **ESTABLISHED:** 1965   **AREA (AC/HA):** 1,280 / 518

DATE(S) VISITED: SPRING ☐   SUMMER ☐   FALL ☐   WINTER ☐

WEATHER: ☀☐ ⛅☐ 🌧☐ ❄☐ ⛈☐ 🌬☐   **TEMP.:**

FEE(S):   RATING: ☆ ☆ ☆ ☆ ☆   **WILL I RETURN?**   YES / NO

LODGING: **WHO I WENT WITH:**

THINGS TO DO: SWIM, FISH, BOAT, STARGAZE, GEOCACHE, CAMP, HIKE

POPULAR ATTRACTIONS:

- Big Oak.
- Lake View Point.

NOTES:

PASSPORT STAMPS

LOCKHART STATE PARK

COUNTY: CALDWELL   **ESTABLISHED:** 1948   **AREA (AC/HA):** 263 / 107

DATE(S) VISITED: SPRING ☐   SUMMER ☐   FALL ☐   WINTER ☐

WEATHER: ☀☐ ☁☐ 🌧☐ ❄☐ ⛈☐ 🌬☐   **TEMP.:**

FEE(S):   RATING: ☆ ☆ ☆ ☆ ☆   **WILL I RETURN?** YES / NO

LODGING: **WHO I WENT WITH:**

THINGS TO DO: SWIM, FISH, GOLF, HIKE, BIKE, CAMP

POPULAR ATTRACTIONS:

- Play golf at the nine-hole golf course built by the Works Progress Administration and the Civilian Conservation Corps over 80 years ago.

NOTES:

PASSPORT STAMPS

LONGHORN CAVERN STATE PARK

COUNTY: BURNET **ESTABLISHED:** 1976 **AREA (AC/HA):** 645 / 261

DATE(S) VISITED: SPRING ☐ SUMMER ☐ FALL ☐ WINTER ☐

WEATHER: ☀☐ ⛅☐ 🌧☐ ❄☐ ⛈☐ 🌬☐ **TEMP.:**

FEE(S): **RATING:** ☆ ☆ ☆ ☆ ☆ **WILL I RETURN?** YES / NO

LODGING: **WHO I WENT WITH:**

THINGS TO DO: HIKE, PICNIC

POPULAR ATTRACTIONS:

- Inks Lake State Park.
- Inks Dam National Fish Hatchery.
- Buchanan Dam (the largest multiarch dam in the world).
- Reveille Peak Ranch.
- Vanishing Texas River Cruise.
- Balcones Canyonlands National Wildlife Refuge.

NOTES:

PASSPORT STAMPS

LOST MAPLES STATE NATURAL AREA

COUNTY: BANDERA, REAL   **ESTABLISHED:** 1979   **AREA (AC/HA):** 2,906 / 1,176

DATE(S) VISITED: SPRING ☐   SUMMER ☐   FALL ☐   WINTER ☐

WEATHER: ☀ ☐ ⛅ ☐ 🌧 ☐ ❄ ☐ ⛈ ☐ 🌬 ☐   **TEMP.:**

FEE(S):   RATING: ☆ ☆ ☆ ☆ ☆   **WILL I RETURN?** YES / NO

LODGING: **WHO I WENT WITH:**

THINGS TO DO: FISH, BIRD WATCH, CAMP, BACKPACK, STARGAZE, GEOCACHE, HIKE

POPULAR ATTRACTIONS:

- Medina Lake.

NOTES:

PASSPORT STAMPS

LYNDON B. JOHNSON STATE PARK & HISTORIC SITE

COUNTY: GILLESPIE   **ESTABLISHED:** 1965   **AREA (AC/HA):** 732 / 297

DATE(S) VISITED: SPRING ☐   SUMMER ☐   FALL ☐   WINTER ☐

WEATHER: ☀ ☐   ⛅ ☐   🌦 ☐   ❄ ☐   🌧 ☐   🌬 ☐   **TEMP.:**

FEE(S):   **RATING:** ☆ ☆ ☆ ☆ ☆   **WILL I RETURN?**   YES / NO

LODGING: **WHO I WENT WITH:**

THINGS TO DO: FISH, TENNIS, BASEBALL, HIKE

POPULAR ATTRACTIONS:

- LBJ's boyhood home and the Lyndon B. Johnson National Historical Park Visitor Center in Johnson City.
- Cluster of stone barns and buildings in Johnson Settlement.
- Pioneer Museum.
- National Museum of the Pacific War.
- Admiral Nimitz Museum.
- George Bush Gallery.

NOTES:

PASSPORT STAMPS

MARTIN CREEK LAKE STATE PARK

COUNTY: RUSK   **ESTABLISHED:** 1976   **AREA (AC/HA):** 286 / 116

DATE(S) VISITED: SPRING ☐ SUMMER ☐ FALL ☐ WINTER ☐

WEATHER: ☀ ☐ ⛅ ☐ 🌧 ☐ ❄ ☐ 🌧 ☐ 🌬 ☐   **TEMP.:**

FEE(S):   RATING: ☆ ☆ ☆ ☆ ☆   **WILL I RETURN?** YES / NO

LODGING: **WHO I WENT WITH:**

THINGS TO DO: FISH, BOAT, CAMP, PADDLE, SWIM, HIKE, BIKE, PICNIC, GEOCACHE, WATER SKI

POPULAR ATTRACTIONS:

- Starr Family Home State Historic Site.
- Texas State Railroad.
- Historic cities of Marshall, Longview, Kilgore, Carthage and Henderson.

NOTES:

PASSPORT STAMPS

MARTIN DIES, JR. STATE PARK

COUNTY: JASPER, TYLER   **ESTABLISHED:** 1965   **AREA (AC/HA):** 730 / 300

DATE(S) VISITED: SPRING ☐   SUMMER ☐   FALL ☐   WINTER ☐

WEATHER: ☀ ☐   ⛅ ☐   🌦 ☐   ❄ ☐   🌧 ☐   🌫 ☐   **TEMP.:**

FEE(S):   RATING: ☆ ☆ ☆ ☆ ☆   **WILL I RETURN?** YES / NO

LODGING: **WHO I WENT WITH:**

THINGS TO DO: PADDLE, BIKE, SWIM, FISH, GEOCACHE

POPULAR ATTRACTIONS:

- Angelina National Forest.
- Big Thicket National Preserve.
- Alabama-Coushatta Tribe Reservation.

NOTES:

PASSPORT STAMPS

MCKINNEY FALLS STATE PARK

COUNTY: TRAVIS   **ESTABLISHED:** 1976   **AREA (AC/HA):** 744 / 301

DATE(S) VISITED: SPRING ☐ SUMMER ☐ FALL ☐ WINTER ☐

WEATHER: ☀☐ ⛅☐ 🌧☐ ❄☐ ⛈☐ 🌬☐   **TEMP.:**

FEE(S):   RATING: ☆ ☆ ☆ ☆ ☆   **WILL I RETURN?** YES / NO

LODGING: **WHO I WENT WITH:**

THINGS TO DO: CAMP, HIKE, MOUNTAIN BIKE, GEOCACHE, PICNIC, SWIM, FISH

POPULAR ATTRACTIONS:

- Hill Country woods.
- Early Texas homestead.

NOTES:

PASSPORT STAMPS

MERIDIAN STATE PARK

COUNTY: BOSQUE   **ESTABLISHED:** 1935   **AREA (AC/HA):** 505 / 204

DATE(S) VISITED: SPRING ☐   SUMMER ☐   FALL ☐   WINTER ☐

WEATHER: ☀️☐ ⛅☐ 🌧️☐ ❄️☐ ⛈️☐ 🌬️☐   **TEMP.:**

FEE(S):   RATING: ☆ ☆ ☆ ☆ ☆   **WILL I RETURN?** YES / NO

LODGING: **WHO I WENT WITH:**

THINGS TO DO: SWIM, PADDLE, PICNIC, CAMP, HIKE, FISH, BIRD WATCH

POPULAR ATTRACTIONS:

- Bosque Hiking Trail.
- Shinnery Ridge Trail.

NOTES:

PASSPORT STAMPS

MISSION TEJAS STATE PARK

COUNTY: HOUSTON   **ESTABLISHED:** 1957   **AREA (AC/HA):** 660 / 270

DATE(S) VISITED: SPRING ☐   SUMMER ☐   FALL ☐   WINTER ☐

WEATHER: ☀☐ ⛅☐ 🌦☐ ❄☐ 🌧☐ 🌬☐   **TEMP.:**

FEE(S):   RATING: ☆ ☆ ☆ ☆ ☆   **WILL I RETURN?**   YES / NO

LODGING: **WHO I WENT WITH:**

THINGS TO DO: HIKE, FISH, CAMP, GEOCACHE

POPULAR ATTRACTIONS:

- Caddo Mounds State Historic Site.
- Varner-Hogg Historic Site.
- Texas State Railroad.
- Davy Crockett National Forest.
- Texas Forestry Museum.
- Ratcliff Lake Recreation Area.

NOTES:

PASSPORT STAMPS

MONAHANS SANDHILLS STATE PARK

COUNTY: WARD, WINKLER   **ESTABLISHED:** 1957   **AREA (AC/HA):** 3,840 / 1,550

DATE(S) VISITED: SPRING ☐   SUMMER ☐   FALL ☐   WINTER ☐

WEATHER: ☀☐ ⛅☐ 🌧☐ ❄☐ ⛈☐ 🌬☐   **TEMP.:**

FEE(S):   RATING: ☆ ☆ ☆ ☆ ☆   **WILL I RETURN?** YES / NO

LODGING: **WHO I WENT WITH:**

THINGS TO DO: PICNIC, HIKE, CAMP

POPULAR ATTRACTIONS:

- Soar down the dunes.

NOTES:

PASSPORT STAMPS

MOTHER NEFF STATE PARK

COUNTY: CORYELL   **ESTABLISHED:** 1937   **AREA (AC/HA):** 259 / 105

DATE(S) VISITED: SPRING ☐ SUMMER ☐ FALL ☐ WINTER ☐

WEATHER: ☀ ☐ ⛅ ☐ 🌧 ☐ ❄ ☐ ⛈ ☐ 🌬 ☐   **TEMP.:**

FEE(S):   RATING: ☆ ☆ ☆ ☆ ☆   **WILL I RETURN?** YES / NO

LODGING: **WHO I WENT WITH:**

THINGS TO DO: HIKE, PICNIC, CAMP, GEOCACHE, SWIM, FISH

POPULAR ATTRACTIONS:

- Texas Ranger Hall of Fame and Museum.
- Cameron Park Zoo.
- Temple Railroad and Heritage Museum.
- Coryell County Museum & Historical Center.

NOTES:

PASSPORT STAMPS

MUSTANG ISLAND STATE PARK

COUNTY: NUECES   **ESTABLISHED:** 1979   **AREA (AC/HA):** 3,954 / 1,600

DATE(S) VISITED: SPRING ☐   SUMMER ☐   FALL ☐   WINTER ☐

WEATHER: ☀ ☐ ⛅ ☐ 🌦 ☐ ❄ ☐ 🌧 ☐ 🌬 ☐   **TEMP.:**

FEE(S):   **RATING:** ☆ ☆ ☆ ☆ ☆   **WILL I RETURN?** YES / NO

LODGING: **WHO I WENT WITH:**

THINGS TO DO: SWIM, SURF, CAMP, PICNIC, FISH, HIKE, MOUNTAIN BIKE, KAYAK, BIRD WATCH

POPULAR ATTRACTIONS:

- Texas State Aquarium.
- USS Lexington.
- Port Aransas.
- Copano Fishing Pier.
- Great Texas Coastal Birding Trail – Central Texas Coast.
- Padre Island National Seashore.
- Aransas National Wildlife Refuge.

NOTES:

PASSPORT STAMPS

OLD TUNNEL STATE PARK

COUNTY: KENDALL   **ESTABLISHED:** 2012   **AREA (AC/HA):** 16 / 6

DATE(S) VISITED: SPRING ☐   SUMMER ☐   FALL ☐   WINTER ☐

WEATHER: ☀☐ ⛅☐ ☁☐ ❄☐ 🌧☐ 🌬☐   **TEMP.:**

FEE(S):   RATING: ☆ ☆ ☆ ☆ ☆   **WILL I RETURN?** YES / NO

LODGING: **WHO I WENT WITH:**

THINGS TO DO: BAT WATCH, HIKE, BIRD WATCH, PICNIC

POPULAR ATTRACTIONS:

- More than 3 million Mexican free-tailed bats.

NOTES:

PASSPORT STAMPS

PALMETTO STATE PARK

COUNTY: GONZALES   **ESTABLISHED:** 1936   **AREA (AC/HA):** 270 / 109

DATE(S) VISITED: SPRING ☐   SUMMER ☐   FALL ☐   WINTER ☐

WEATHER: ☀ ☐   ⛅ ☐   🌧 ☐   ❄ ☐   🌧 ☐   🌬 ☐   **TEMP.:**

FEE(S):   RATING: ☆ ☆ ☆ ☆ ☆   **WILL I RETURN?**   YES / NO

LODGING: **WHO I WENT WITH:**

THINGS TO DO: SWIM, FISH, CANOE, HIKE, BIKE, GEOCACHE, PADDLE

POPULAR ATTRACTIONS:

- Luling Oil Museum.
- Lockhart, the official Barbecue Capital of Texas.

NOTES:

PASSPORT STAMPS

PALO DURO CANYON STATE PARK

COUNTY: RANDALL   **ESTABLISHED:** 1934   **AREA (AC/HA):** 28,000 / 11,331

DATE(S) VISITED: SPRING ☐   SUMMER ☐   FALL ☐   WINTER ☐

WEATHER: ☀ ☐   ⛅ ☐   🌧 ☐   ❄ ☐   ⛈ ☐   🌬 ☐   **TEMP.:**

FEE(S):   RATING: ☆ ☆ ☆ ☆ ☆   **WILL I RETURN?**   YES / NO

LODGING: **WHO I WENT WITH:**

THINGS TO DO: HIKE, MOUNTAIN BIKE, BIKE, CAMP, GEOCACHE, BIRD WATCH

POPULAR ATTRACTIONS:

- Panhandle-Plains Historical Museum.
- Buffalo Lake National Wildlife Refuge.
- Amarillo Zoo.
- Don Harrington Discovery Center.
- Wildcat Bluff Nature Center.
- American Quarter Horse Hall of Fame & Museum.
- Lake Meredith National Recreation Area.
- Alibates Flint Quarries National Monument.

NOTES:

PASSPORT STAMPS

PEDERNALES FALLS STATE PARK

COUNTY: BLANCO   **ESTABLISHED:** 1971   **AREA (AC/HA):** 5,211 / 2,109

DATE(S) VISITED: SPRING ☐   SUMMER ☐   FALL ☐   WINTER ☐

WEATHER: ☀☐ ⛅☐ 🌧☐ ❄☐ 🌧☐ 🌬☐   **TEMP.:**

FEE(S):   RATING: ☆ ☆ ☆ ☆ ☆   **WILL I RETURN?** YES / NO

LODGING: **WHO I WENT WITH:**

THINGS TO DO: CAMP, HIKE, MOUNTAIN BIKE, PICNIC, GEOCACHE, BIRD WATCH, SWIM, FISH

POPULAR ATTRACTIONS:

- Art galleries and museums in Johnson City.
- Lyndon B. Johnson National Historical Park.
- Lyndon B. John State Park & Historic Site.

NOTES:

PASSPORT STAMPS

POSSUM KINGDOM STATE PARK

COUNTY: PALO PINTO   **ESTABLISHED:** 1940   **AREA (AC/HA):** 1,528 / 618

DATE(S) VISITED: SPRING ☐ SUMMER ☐ FALL ☐ WINTER ☐

WEATHER: ☀☐ ⛅☐ ☁☐ ❄☐ 🌧☐ 🌬☐ **TEMP.:**

FEE(S):   RATING: ☆ ☆ ☆ ☆ ☆   **WILL I RETURN?**   YES / NO

LODGING: **WHO I WENT WITH:**

THINGS TO DO: SWIM, BOAT, FISH, WATER SKI, SCUBA DIVE, SNORKEL, CAMP, PICNIC, HIKE, BIKE

POPULAR ATTRACTIONS:

- Possum Kingdom Lake.

NOTES:

PASSPORT STAMPS

PURTIS CREEK STATE PARK

COUNTY: HENDERSON, VAN ZANDT   **ESTABLISHED:** 1988   **AREA (AC/HA):** 1,582 / 640

DATE(S) VISITED: SPRING ☐   SUMMER ☐   FALL ☐   WINTER ☐

WEATHER: ☀☐ ⛅☐ 🌧☐ ❄☐ ⛈☐ 🌬☐   **TEMP.:**

FEE(S):   RATING: ☆ ☆ ☆ ☆ ☆   **WILL I RETURN?** YES / NO

LODGING: **WHO I WENT WITH:**

THINGS TO DO: BOAT, HIKE, BIKE. CAMP, GEOCACHE, PICNIC, FISH

POPULAR ATTRACTIONS:

- Museums in Athens.
- Texas Freshwater Fisheries Center.
- Cedar Creek Reservoir.

NOTES:

PASSPORT STAMPS

RAY ROBERTS LAKE STATE PARK

COUNTY: DENTON, COOKE, GRAYSON **ESTABLISHED:** 1993 **AREA (AC/HA):** 29,350 / 11,880

DATE(S) VISITED: SPRING ☐ SUMMER ☐ FALL ☐ WINTER ☐

WEATHER: ☀️☐ ☁️☐ 🌦️☐ ❄️☐ 🌧️☐ 🌫️☐ **TEMP.:**

FEE(S): RATING: ☆ ☆ ☆ ☆ ☆ **WILL I RETURN?** YES / NO

LODGING: **WHO I WENT WITH:**

THINGS TO DO: CAMP, HIKE, BIKE, GEOCACHE, BACKPACK, PADDLE, FISH, SWIM

POPULAR ATTRACTIONS:

- Denton: Museums, art galleries, restaurants and more.
- Gainesville: Morton Museum, antique shops and zoo.
- Collinsville: Antique shopping and historical landmarks.
- Fort Worth.
- Eisenhower Birthplace State Historic Site.

NOTES:

PASSPORT STAMPS

RESACA DE LA PALMA STATE PARK

COUNTY: CAMERON   **ESTABLISHED:** 2008   **AREA (AC/HA):** 1,200 / 490

DATE(S) VISITED: SPRING ☐ SUMMER ☐ FALL ☐ WINTER ☐

WEATHER: ☀☐ ⛅☐ 🌧☐ ❄☐ ⛈☐ 🌬☐   **TEMP.:**

FEE(S):   RATING: ☆ ☆ ☆ ☆ ☆   **WILL I RETURN?** YES / NO

LODGING: **WHO I WENT WITH:**

THINGS TO DO: TRAM, HIKE, BIKE, BIRD WATCH

POPULAR ATTRACTIONS:

- Butterfly garden.

NOTES:

PASSPORT STAMPS

SAN ANGELO STATE PARK

COUNTY: TOM GREEN   **ESTABLISHED:** 1995   **AREA (AC/HA):** 7,677 / 3,107

DATE(S) VISITED: SPRING ☐   SUMMER ☐   FALL ☐   WINTER ☐

WEATHER: ☀ ☐ ⛅ ☐ 🌧 ☐ ❄ ☐ ⛈ ☐ 🌫 ☐   **TEMP.:**

FEE(S):   RATING: ☆ ☆ ☆ ☆ ☆   **WILL I RETURN?** YES / NO

LODGING: **WHO I WENT WITH:**

THINGS TO DO: CAMP, HIKE, BIKE, RIDE HORSE, GEOCACHE, FISH, SWIM, BOAT, PADDLE

POPULAR ATTRACTIONS:

- Fort Concho.
- Lake Nasworthy.
- Twin Buttes Reservoir.

NOTES:

PASSPORT STAMPS

SEA RIM STATE PARK

COUNTY: JEFFERSON   **ESTABLISHED:** 1977   **AREA (AC/HA):** 4,141 / 1,676

DATE(S) VISITED: SPRING ☐ SUMMER ☐ FALL ☐ WINTER ☐

WEATHER: ☀ ☐ ⛅ ☐ 🌧 ☐ ❄ ☐ 🌧 ☐ 🌬 ☐   **TEMP.:**

FEE(S):   RATING: ☆ ☆ ☆ ☆ ☆   **WILL I RETURN?** YES / NO

LODGING: **WHO I WENT WITH:**

THINGS TO DO: CAMP, BIRD WATCH, PADDLE, SWIM, FISH, HUNT

POPULAR ATTRACTIONS:

- McFaddin National Wildlife Refuge.
- J.D. Murphree Wildlife Management Area.
- Sabine Pass Battleground.
- Big Thicket National Preserve.
- Port Arthur.

NOTES:

PASSPORT STAMPS

SEMINOLE CANYON STATE PARK & HISTORIC SITE

COUNTY: VAL VERDE   **ESTABLISHED:** 1980   **AREA (AC/HA):** 2,172 / 879

DATE(S) VISITED: SPRING ☐ SUMMER ☐ FALL ☐ WINTER ☐

WEATHER: ☀ ☐ ☁ ☐ 🌧 ☐ ❄ ☐ 🌧 ☐ 🌬 ☐   **TEMP.:**

FEE(S):   RATING: ☆ ☆ ☆ ☆ ☆   **WILL I RETURN?** YES / NO

LODGING: **WHO I WENT WITH:**

THINGS TO DO: CAMP, HIKE, MOUNTAIN BIKE, GEOCACHE

POPULAR ATTRACTIONS:

- Del Rio offers restaurants, lodging and access to outdoor activities.
- Ciudad Acuna.
- Amistad Reservoir.
- Amistad National Recreation Area.
- Judge Roy Bean Visitor Center.

NOTES:

PASSPORT STAMPS

SHELDON LAKE STATE PARK & ENVIRONMENTAL LEARNING CENTER

COUNTY: HARRIS   **ESTABLISHED:** 1984   **AREA (AC/HA):** 1,200 / 485

DATE(S) VISITED: SPRING ☐   SUMMER ☐   FALL ☐   WINTER ☐

WEATHER: ☀☐ ⛅☐ 🌦☐ ❄☐ 🌧☐ 🌫☐   **TEMP.:**

FEE(S):   RATING: ☆ ☆ ☆ ☆ ☆   **WILL I RETURN?** YES / NO

LODGING: **WHO I WENT WITH:**

THINGS TO DO: FISH, BOAT, BIRD WATCH, HIKE

POPULAR ATTRACTIONS:

- San Jacinto Battleground Historic Complex.
- Lake Houston Park.
- NASA's Johnson Space Center.
- Mercer Arboretum.
- Houston Zoological Gardens.
- Houston Museum District.

NOTES:

PASSPORT STAMPS

SOUTH LLANO RIVER STATE PARK

COUNTY: KIMBLE   **ESTABLISHED:** 1990   **AREA (AC/HA):** 2,600 / 1052

DATE(S) VISITED: SPRING ☐   SUMMER ☐   FALL ☐   WINTER ☐

WEATHER: ☐ ☐ ☐ ☐ ☐ ☐   **TEMP.:**

FEE(S):   **RATING:** ☆ ☆ ☆ ☆ ☆   **WILL I RETURN?** YES / NO

LODGING: **WHO I WENT WITH:**

THINGS TO DO: SWIM, PADDLE, FISH, CAMP, HIKE, BIKE, GEOCACHE, STARGAZE, BIRD WATCH

POPULAR ATTRACTIONS:

- Views of the Texas Hill Country.
- Devil's Sinkhole State Natural Area.
- Stellar views of the night sky, including the Milky Way.

NOTES:

PASSPORT STAMPS

STEPHEN F. AUSTIN STATE PARK

COUNTY: AUSTIN   **ESTABLISHED:** 1940   **AREA (AC/HA):** 663 / 268

DATE(S) VISITED: SPRING ☐   SUMMER ☐   FALL ☐   WINTER ☐

WEATHER: ☀ ☐   ⛅ ☐   🌧 ☐   ❄ ☐   ⛈ ☐   🌬 ☐   **TEMP.:**

FEE(S):   RATING: ☆ ☆ ☆ ☆ ☆   **WILL I RETURN?** YES / NO

LODGING: **WHO I WENT WITH:**

THINGS TO DO: PICNIC, GEOCACHE, CAMP, HIKE, BIKE

POPULAR ATTRACTIONS:

- San Felipe de Austin State Historic Site.
- Stephen F. Austin Golf Course.

NOTES:

PASSPORT STAMPS

TYLER STATE PARK

COUNTY: SMITH   **ESTABLISHED:** 1939   **AREA (AC/HA):** 985 / 399

DATE(S) VISITED: SPRING ☐   SUMMER ☐   FALL ☐   WINTER ☐

WEATHER: ☀ ☐   ⛅ ☐   🌧 ☐   ❄ ☐   🌧 ☐   🌬 ☐   **TEMP.:**

FEE(S):   RATING: ☆ ☆ ☆ ☆ ☆   **WILL I RETURN?**   YES / NO

LODGING: **WHO I WENT WITH:**

THINGS TO DO: BOAT, FISH, SWIM, HIKE, MOUNTAIN BIKE, PICNIC, GEOCACHE, CAMP, BIRD WATCH

POPULAR ATTRACTIONS:

- Discovery Science Place.
- Azalea Trail (March).
- Rose Festival (October).
- Texas Freshwater Fisheries Center in Athens.
- East Texas Oil Museum in Kilgore.
- Salt Palace Museum in Grand Saline.

NOTES:

PASSPORT STAMPS

VILLAGE CREEK STATE PARK

COUNTY: HARDIN   **ESTABLISHED:** 1994   **AREA (AC/HA):** 1,090 / 441

DATE(S) VISITED: SPRING ☐   SUMMER ☐   FALL ☐   WINTER ☐

WEATHER: ☀☐ ⛅☐ 🌧☐ ❄☐ ⛈☐ 🌬☐   **TEMP.:**

FEE(S):   RATING: ☆ ☆ ☆ ☆ ☆   **WILL I RETURN?**   YES / NO

LODGING: **WHO I WENT WITH:**

THINGS TO DO: CAMP, PICNIC, FISH, HIKE, MOUNTAIN BIKE, SWIM, GEOCACHE

POPULAR ATTRACTIONS:

- Big Thicket National Preserve.
- Roy E. Larsen Sandyland Sanctuary.

NOTES:

PASSPORT STAMPS

WYLER AERIAL TRAMWAY

COUNTY: EL PASO   **ESTABLISHED:** 2001   **AREA (AC/HA):** 196 / 79

DATE(S) VISITED: SPRING ☐ SUMMER ☐ FALL ☐ WINTER ☐

WEATHER: ☀☐ ⛅☐ ☁☐ ❄☐ 🌧☐ 🌬☐   **TEMP.:**

FEE(S):   RATING: ☆ ☆ ☆ ☆ ☆   **WILL I RETURN?** YES / NO

LODGING: **WHO I WENT WITH:**

THINGS TO DO: BIRD WATCH, HIKE

POPULAR ATTRACTIONS:

- The tramway was closed indefinitely to the public in September 2018.

NOTES:

PASSPORT STAMPS

PHOTOS   PARK NAME..

PHOTOS   PARK NAME..

PHOTOS   PARK NAME..

PHOTOS   PARK NAME...

PHOTOS   PARK NAME...

PHOTOS   PARK NAME...

PHOTOS   PARK NAME...

PHOTOS   PARK NAME..

PHOTOS   PARK NAME...

PHOTOS   PARK NAME...

Thank you for purchasing my book!
I hope you enjoyed it!
If you do, would you consider posting an
online review?

This helps me to continue providing great
products and helps potential buyers to make
confident decisions.

Thank you in advance for your review.

Write to me if you think I should improve anything
in my book:

maxkukisgalgan@gmail.com

Max Kukis Galgan

SEE OTHER BOOKS

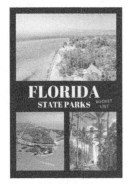

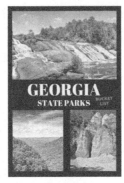

Made in the USA
Coppell, TX
28 September 2023

22161534R00066